Big
Science Ideas

Nature's Cleaners

Bobbie Kalman

Crabtree Publishing Company

www.crabtreebooks.com

Big Science Ideas

Created by Bobbie Kalman

For John and Mary George,
Our favorite "opportunistic-feeding-nature-cleaning" partners
We have scavenged and decomposed many meals together with gusto!

Author and Editor-in-Chief
Bobbie Kalman

Text and photo research
Crystal Sikkens

Editor
Kathy Middleton

Design
Bobbie Kalman
Katherine Kantor
Samantha Crabtree (cover)

Production coordinator
Katherine Kantor

Prepress technician
Margaret Amy Salter

Illustrations
Barbara Bedell: front cover, pages 18 (middle and right worm),
    27 (mushrooms), 28-29
Katherine Kantor: page 14
Robert MacGregor: page 13 (top right beetle)
Bonna Rouse: page 27 (roots)
Margaret Amy Salter: page 18 (left worm)

Photographs
© Dreamstime.com: pages 14 (maggots), 20 (left)
© iStockphoto.com: front cover (slug), pages 11 (bottom),
    15 (bottom left), 19, 30 (right)
© Shutterstock.com: front cover (mushrooms and worm),
    back cover, title page, pages 3, 4, 5, 6, 7, 8, 9, 10, 11 (top),
    12, 13 (except top right beetle), 14 (except maggots),
    15 (except bottom left), 16, 17, 18, 20 (right), 21, 22, 23,
    24, 25, 26 (except top left), 28, 29, 30 (left), 31
Other images by Photodisc

Library and Archives Canada Cataloguing in Publication

Kalman, Bobbie, 1947-
    Nature's cleaners / Bobbie Kalman.

(Big science ideas)
Includes index.
ISBN 978-0-7787-3280-8 (bound).--ISBN 978-0-7787-3300-3 (pbk.)

    1. Biodegradation--Juvenile literature. 2. Scavengers (Zoology)--
Juvenile literature. I. Title. II. Series: Kalman, Bobbie, 1947- . Big.
science ideas.

QL756.5.K343 2008   j577'.16   C2008-905728-7

Library of Congress Cataloging-in-Publication Data

Kalman, Bobbie.
    Nature's cleaners / Bobbie Kalman.
        p. cm. -- (Big science ideas)
    Includes index.
    ISBN-13: 978-0-7787-3300-3 (pbk. : alk. paper)
    ISBN-10: 0-7787-3300-9 (pbk. : alk. paper)
    ISBN-13: 978-0-7787-3280-8 (reinforced library binding : alk. paper)
    ISBN-10: 0-7787-3280-0 (reinforced library binding : alk. paper)
    1. Scavengers (Zoology)--Juvenile literature. 2. Biodegradation--
Juvenile literature. I. Title.
    QL756.5.K356 2009
    577'.16--dc22
                                                2008037687

Crabtree Publishing Company

www.crabtreebooks.com   1-800-387-7650

Published in Canada
Crabtree Publishing
616 Welland Ave.
St. Catharines, Ontario
L2M 5V6

Published in the United States
Crabtree Publishing
PMB16A
350 Fifth Ave., Suite 3308
New York, NY 10118

Published in the United Kingdom
Crabtree Publishing
White Cross Mills
High Town, Lancaster
LA1 4XS

Published in Australia
Crabtree Publishing
386 Mt. Alexander Rd.
Ascot Vale (Melbourne)
VIC 3032

Contents

Living things and energy

Mushrooms are fungi.

Plants, animals, and people are **living things**. There are other living things, too. **Fungi** and **bacteria** are living things. **Molds** and mushrooms are two kinds of fungi. Bacteria are tiny living things. They are so small that you can see them only through a microscope.

mold

Molds are fungi, too.

bacteria seen with a microscope

Bacteria are tiny living things.

microscope

4

Plants make their own food

All living things need **energy**. Energy is the power living things need to breathe, grow, move, and stay alive. Plants get energy from the sun. They are the only living things that can make food from sunlight. Making food from sunlight is called **photosynthesis**. These plants are using photosynthesis to make food for themselves. This girl can not make food from sunlight. How does she get energy?

What are food chains?

People and animals need to eat food to get energy. The energy of the sun is passed along in food. It is passed from living thing to living thing in **food chains**. This squirrel is eating part of a plant. The plant contains the sun's energy. The energy is now in the squirrel's body. The squirrel is a **consumer**. Consumers **consume**, or eat, food.

Almost all energy comes from the sun.

Plants use the sun's energy to make food. Living things that can make food are called **producers**. *Plants are producers.*

Passing along energy

A hungry fox has now caught the squirrel and will soon eat it. The energy that was in the squirrel, which came from the plant and the sun, will be passed along to the fox. The fox will not eat all of the squirrel, however. It may leave behind some meat, fur, and bones. What will happen to the energy in the rest of that food?

*The squirrel was the **primary**, or first, consumer in the food chain. The fox is a **secondary**, or second, consumer.*

What do animals eat?

Deer are herbivores.

Animals eat different kinds of foods. Animals that eat mainly plants are called **herbivores**. Animals that eat mainly other animals are called **carnivores**. Some animals eat both plants and animals. They are called **omnivores**. Some omnivores are **opportunistic feeders**. Opportunistic feeders eat any food they find.

Raccoons are opportunistic feeders. They eat plants, frogs, birds, insects, and garbage.

Predators and prey

Carnivores eat mainly meat. Some carnivores hunt animals and then eat them. Carnivores that hunt are called **predators**. The animals they hunt are called **prey**. Some carnivores do not hunt. They eat parts of animals that predators have hunted and killed. What are these animals called?

Lions are predators. They hunt large prey. This lion is hunting a wildebeest.

Jackals hunt small prey, but they also eat large prey that other predators, such as lions, have killed.

9

Eating the leftovers

vulture

After predators have eaten enough, part of the prey may be left behind. **Scavengers** find these **remains**, or leftovers. They eat the **carcasses**, or dead bodies of animals. Jackals, hyenas, and vultures are scavengers that live on the **savanna**.

hyena

Lions have killed this wildebeest on the savanna, but they did not eat it all. Some black-backed jackals and a brown hyena have come to feed on the leftovers.

jackal

A spotted hyena will feed on the wildebeest, too. Both jackals and hyenas are scavengers, but they also hunt.

Nature's cleaners

When living things die, they still have energy and **nutrients** in their bodies. The leftover energy and nutrients are used by other living things. Nothing is wasted in nature! Living things that eat dead things help clean the Earth. There are three groups of cleaners in nature. They are scavengers, **detrivores**, and **decomposers**. Scavengers are the first group of nature's cleaners.

The jackals have left. The hyena and some vultures are now eating the wildebeest carcass. Vultures are scavengers that do not hunt.

11

Scavenger habitats

Jackals, hyenas, vultures, and marabou storks are scavengers on the savanna, but there are scavengers in every **habitat** on Earth. A habitat is the natural home of plants, animals, and other living things. There are scavengers in **forests**, **deserts**, **grasslands**, as well as in rivers, lakes, and oceans. Scavengers also find food on **shores**. Shores are the edges of lakes and oceans.

vulture

Marabou storks find food on land and on the shores of oceans.
*They have long legs for **wading**. Wading is walking through water.*

Burying beetles are forest and grassland scavengers. When a male and female burying beetle find a dead bird or mouse, they cover its body with dirt. The female then lays eggs in the soil near the carcass. When the eggs hatch, the parents feed parts of the carcass to the **larvae**, or babies.

Burying beetles have bright orange bands.

Some lobsters, crabs, and shrimps are scavengers in oceans. Spiny lobsters, such as this one, look for food among the rocks on ocean bottoms.

Some gulls live near oceans, but others live in different habitats. This gull is eating a salmon carcass it has found in a river.

What is detritus?

Detritus is the remains of animals, such as skin, hair, bones, and **feces**. Animals that eat detritus are called detrivores, detritivores, or detritus feeders. They make up nature's second cleaning crew. Some detrivores eat the parts of animals that scavengers have left behind. Other detrivores eat dead plants.

These termites are eating rotting wood.

maggots

***Maggots** are eating the remains of this dead mouse. Maggots are the larvae of flies.*

Detrivores

Detrivores include termites, flies, millipedes, some crabs, dung beetles, cockroaches, snails, slugs, wasps, and earthworms. Some detrivores eat **dung**. Dung is animal feces. It contains nutrients and energy, too. Nothing in nature is wasted.

Dung beetles eat dung. They roll it into balls and take it to their homes.

Millipedes eat parts of dead plants.

Cockroaches eat almost anything they find. They often eat leftover foods in garbage cans.

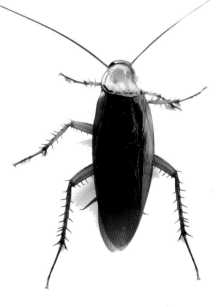

15

Land snails and slugs

Snails are animals with shells. Some snails live on land, and some live in water. Land snails eat live plants, but they also eat detritus such as dead grasses, leaves, and tree bark. Snails have two pairs of **antennae**, or feelers, on their heads. The eyes are on the longer antennae. The short antennae are used for feeling and smelling.

antennae

shell

No shells

Slugs are like snails, but they have no shells. Both snails and slugs are covered in **mucus**, or slime. The mucus allows them to move more easily. Banana slugs are true detrivores. They eat animal feces and dead plant material. They then recycle the nutrients in their waste, which goes into the soil. The leftover nutrients help new plants grow.

Both snails and slugs move on a single foot, which is under their bodies.

Sharp tongues

Both snails and slugs have a **radula** inside their mouths. The radula is like a tongue, but it has many tiny teeth. Snails and slugs use the radula like a saw and scrape pieces of food off with it.

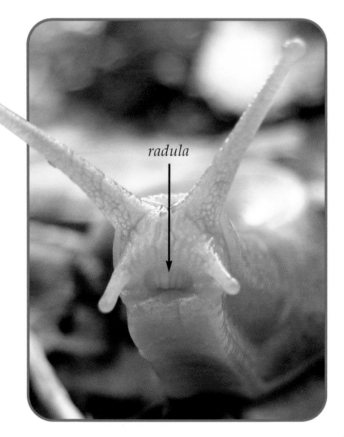

Worms in the soil

Earthworms are detrivores that play a very important role in keeping nature clean and healthy. They eat soil. Soil contains pieces of dead plants and animals. Instead of teeth, earthworms have strong muscles in their mouths that suck up this detritus in the soil. They use the nutrients in the detritus and put the leftover nutrients back into the soil. The nutrients are in their **castings**, or waste. Castings help plants grow.

Tunnels of air and water

Earthworms also help plants by digging tunnels in the ground as they eat soil. The tunnels allow air and water, which plant roots need, to get into the soil more easily. The tunnels also make more room for roots to grow deeper. Plants with deep roots are healthier.

roots

tunnels

Ocean cleaners

There are detrivores in oceans, too. Sea cucumbers are a lot like earthworms. They suck in sand at the bottom of oceans. The sand is full of detritus. Sea cucumbers take the nutrients from the detritus. They leave behind strings of waste in the sand, similar to the castings that earthworms leave in soil. The waste is eaten by other creatures.

Some ocean animals with shells, such as this conch, also eat detritus.

Feather stars

Feather stars have feather-like arms that trap the detritus that floats in ocean water. Some have five arms, others have as many as 200 arms. The arms are coated with a sticky mucus that helps catch small bits of food in the water. Feather stars often attach themselves to rocks or corals, but they can also move from place to place.

What are decomposers?

Decomposers are the last group of nature's cleaners. To **decompose** means to take apart. Decomposers take apart dead things and **recycle**, or change, them so they can be used in other ways. Detrivores are animals, but decomposers are neither plants nor animals. They are different kinds of living things. Bacteria and fungi are the two main types of decomposers. Mushrooms, yeasts, and molds are fungi.

What is the name that people use to describe mushrooms that are poisonous? Does this toad give you a clue? Did you guess that the name is toadstool?

What is bacteria?

Bacteria are among the smallest living things on Earth, but they are very important decomposers. Bacteria are everywhere! You have billions of helpful bacteria on and inside your body. Your food also contains bacteria. Foods such as yogurt contain good bacteria that your body needs.

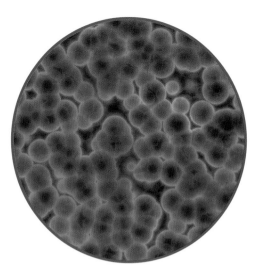

You cannot see bacteria without a microscope.

Good bacteria help break down foods inside your body. Other kinds of bacteria, however, can make you very sick!

yogurt

23

Yeasts and molds

This girl has used yeast to make bread. Yeast produces gas, which makes bread rise.

Yeasts and molds are fungi. Fungi cannot make their own food the way plants can. Most fungi are not **visible**, or able to be seen, by the naked eye. They live mainly in the soil and in dead things. Fungi take nutrients from dead plants and animals and recycle them. They make waste usable again.

Yeast and bread

Some yeasts are used in making food. Most kinds of bread are made with yeast. Yeast makes bread rise. Some yeasts, however, are harmful to living things.

Molds

Molds are fungi, too. They also play a big role in decomposing dead plants and animals. Molds spoil food and break it down quickly. Some molds are used to make foods, drinks, and medicines.

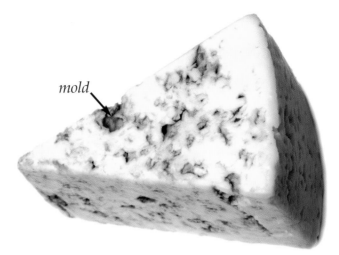

mold

You can see the blue mold in this piece of blue cheese. Many people like the taste of this cheese.

This bread has two kinds of fungi. It was made with yeast, and now it is covered in mold. If you ate this bread, you would probably get sick.

Some people have trouble breathing around molds. There are molds that can make people very sick.

25

Helpful mushrooms

Mushrooms are fungi that can be found all over forests. They are the most important forest decomposers because they are the only ones that can break down tough dead wood. There are thousands of different kinds of mushrooms. Some can be eaten, and others are poisonous. The red mushrooms below are toadstools. Eating them could cause illness or even death.

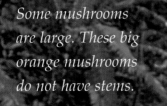

Some mushrooms are large. These big orange mushrooms do not have stems.

Mushroom parts

Mushrooms and other fungi make **spores** instead of seeds. Mushrooms make spores in their **gills**. Some mushrooms are joined together under the ground by threads called **hyphae**. Hyphae are like thin roots. They connect with the roots of plants and help plants get more water and nutrients from the soil.

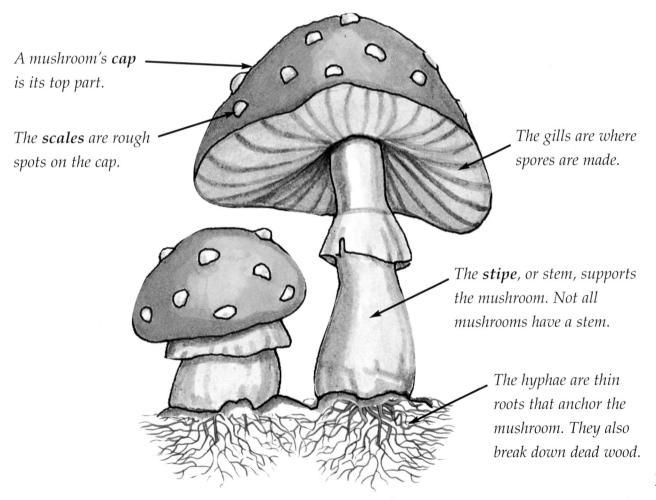

A mushroom's **cap** is its top part.

The **scales** are rough spots on the cap.

The gills are where spores are made.

The **stipe**, or stem, supports the mushroom. Not all mushrooms have a stem.

The hyphae are thin roots that anchor the mushroom. They also break down dead wood.

Energy keeps going

The food chain on pages 6 and 7 shows how animals must eat food to get nutrients and energy. Nutrients and energy are passed along in food. They are passed from living thing to living thing in food chains. Food chains are made up of the sun, plants, herbivores, and carnivores. Carnivores do not eat every part of an animal, however. There are parts that are left. This food chain shows how the nutrients and energy in leftovers are passed along after carnivores have finished eating.

Lions hunted and killed this wildebeest. Lions are predators and carnivores.

These jackals are eating some of the leftovers. Jackals are carnivores called scavengers.

Scavengers

Jackals, hyenas, and vultures belong to the first group of nature's cleaners.

striped hyena

jackal

vulture

Detrivores

Dung beetles, termites, worms, and millipedes belong to the second group of nature's cleaners.

termite

dung beetle

millipede

earthworm

Decomposers

Mushrooms, molds, and bacteria belong to the final group of nature's cleaners.

mold

mushrooms

bacteria

29

People eat it all!

People eat vegetables.

Some people are **vegetarians** that eat only fruits and vegetables, but most people are omnivores. Omnivores eat every kind of food. They eat plants, herbivores, carnivores, scavengers, detrivores, and decomposers. Are you an omnivore, a herbivore, or a picky eater?

We eat all kinds of meat, too.

This girl is eating a lamb kebab. Lambs are herbivores. Most of the meat we eat comes from herbivores.

30

Some people love seafood, such as these spiny lobsters. Spiny lobsters are scavengers.

Have you ever tasted cooked snails? Snails are detrivores.

Yogurt has a lot of good bacteria. Bacteria are decomposers.

This mushroom sandwich has two kinds of fungi—yeast and mushrooms. Both mushrooms and yeast are decomposers.

Are you a "nature's cleaner?" Do you eat scavengers, detrivores, and decomposers? Make a list of the foods you eat.

31

Glossary

Note: Some boldfaced words are defined where they appear in the book.

bacteria Tiny living things that are made of one cell and which break down dead things; bacteria can also cause diseases

desert A dry area of land that gets little rain or snow and where few plants grow

feces Waste that comes from a human or an animal's body

forest A large area that is covered with trees and other plants

fungus (fungi) Any of the group of living things that breaks down dead matter, such as mushrooms, yeasts, and molds

gills The plates on the underside of a mushroom, where spores are made

grassland A large open area of land that is covered with grass

living thing Something or someone that is alive and needs air, light, water, and food

mold A furry-looking fungus that lives in damp places and is often found on food

nutrient An important part of food that helps living things stay healthy

savanna A hot grassland with a few trees

spore A small part of a fungus or other simple living thing, which can grow into another living thing like it

Index

Printed in the U.S.A. - CG